T0149566

Foundations for Flourishing

Inspirations and intentional actions to positively influence your wellbeing

Nicole Shanks

BALBOA. PRESS

A DIVISION OF HAY HOUSE

Copyright © 2019 Nicole Shanks.

All rights reserved. No part of this book may be used or reproduced by any means, graphic, electronic, or mechanical, including photocopying, recording, taping or by any information storage retrieval system without the written permission of the author except in the case of brief quotations embodied in critical articles and reviews.

Balboa Press books may be ordered through booksellers or by contacting:

Balboa Press
A Division of Hay House
1663 Liberty Drive
Bloomington, IN 47403
www.balboapress.com.au
1 (877) 407-4847

Because of the dynamic nature of the Internet, any web addresses or links contained in this book may have changed since publication and may no longer be valid. The views expressed in this work are solely those of the author and do not necessarily reflect the views of the publisher, and the publisher hereby disclaims any responsibility for them.

The author of this book does not dispense medical advice or prescribe the use of any technique as a form of treatment for physical, emotional, or medical problems without the advice of a physician, either directly or indirectly. The intent of the author is only to offer information of a general nature to help you in your quest for emotional and spiritual well-being. In the event you use any of the information in this book for yourself, which is your constitutional right, the author and the publisher assume no responsibility for your actions.

Any people depicted in stock imagery provided by Getty Images are models,
and such images are being used for illustrative purposes only.
Certain stock imagery © Getty Images.

ISBN: 978-1-5043-1865-5 (sc)
ISBN: 978-1-5043-1867-9 (e)

Print information available on the last page.

Balboa Press rev. date: 07/20/2019

Contents

Introduction

The path to a flourishing well-being is not without diversions, bumps, and ruts. I have many clients who have, at one time or another, come to me and said that they felt like they were swimming against the tide, like they were on the hamster wheel of life. And for the most part, they report not knowing where to start to make a change.

When we "unpack" what is going on for them, it is often times a case of what I call "the empty cup."

When we are focussed on caring for others, doing well at our jobs, and saying yes to please our family, friends, and co-workers, we can often forget ourselves and neglect our needs. When we are faced with trying times, we might get stuck in patterns of rumination, of speaking to ourselves unkindly, of expecting too much. Our negative thought patterns can grow stronger. It happens incrementally, over time. Before we know it, we might feel disconnected, flat. We look back instead of living in the now. We do not show up each day as our best selves.

It was after considering the number of people who walk into my coaching clinic with cups heading towards empty that I decided to create this journal. This interactive resource contains inspirations, intentions, affirmations, reflections, and intentional actions that are geared towards "filling your cup," improving and maintaining your well-being, and guiding you towards a flourishing life.

The aim of this journal is to build your intentional actions to enhance your wellbeing. To guide you in activities that you can use in your endeavours to create a positive and flourishing life.

Set out for you to interact with over twelve weeks, this is a tool that will help you to build your resources, strengthen your mindset, improve your resilience, and focus on your positive path to well-being.

Drawing upon my studies and experience in integrative wellness coaching, positive psychology, and meditation and mindfulness teaching, I have put together a twelve-week program of resources/activities that will create positive habits in your life to help you fill your cup and build a solid foundation as you continue on your journey to a flourishing well-being.

Following are descriptions of the parts of this journal. Incorporating them into your flourishing journey will help you develop the skills needed to find the well-being you seek.

Intentions

An intention is the thought process that precedes an action. Every action that we take is preceded by an intention. When our goal is building and maintaining a positive state of well-being, there are actions that need to take place to achieve that goal.

Setting intentions allows us to take the step from a thought process to an action process. Setting positive intentions influences our behaviours and actions in a positive way.

Use the intention space to state your intentions for the week. Read back over it each day to remind yourself of the intention you have set and to strengthen your commitment to taking action towards your desired goals.

Affirmations

An affirmation is a positive statement that affirms something that is true and valid. Included in this journal are weekly affirmations that describe positive thoughts and actions. Repeating these affirmations daily is a powerful way of positively affecting your mood, state of mind, and belief in achieving your desired state of well-being.

These affirmations will influence the thoughts that you have and the actions that you will take in your daily life that will ultimately lead to a flourishing well-being and a full cup.

Reflections

Use the reflections pages to journal your experiences over the week. Journaling helps to create connections between thoughts, feelings, and behaviours, giving you insight into your why and how. It can help to clear your mind, freeing it from cycling through thoughts that may prevent you from living in the moment.

Write down your positive emotions and experiences from the week too. This will create a space that you can come back to in order to savour those positive emotions.

Gratitude Journal

Gratitude, appreciation, thanks, recognition, acknowledgement, appreciation. Expressing the emotion of gratitude is one of the vital foundations of a flourishing well-being. Writing down our gratitude is associated with increased well-being, happiness and optimism, and higher life satisfaction.

You have the space to record your top three gratitudes for each day over the next twelve weeks. Take time to revisit your gratitude lists, and savour the positive emotions and experiences that are reflected there.

Gratitude Prompts

- Learning from a difficult experience
- Having a need met
- Someone helping you
- Experiencing kindness or compassion
- Overcoming challenges
- Experiencing success
- Spending time with loved ones
- Practising self-care
- Encountering something that has made you laugh or smile
- Visiting a special place
- Feeling accomplished
- Feeling inspired
- Experiencing beauty in your world

Week 1

Intentions

_____

_____

_____

_____

_____

_____

_____

_____

Inspiration

Knowing is not enough; we must apply. Wishing is not enough; we must do.

Johann Wolfgang von Goethe

Affirmation

I am grateful for all that I have and for all that I am.

My Top Three Gratitudes

Monday

1.

2.

3.

Tuesday

1.

2.

3.

Wednesday

1.

2.

3.

Thursday

1.

2.

3.

Friday

1.

2.

3.

Saturday

1.

2.

3.

Sunday

1.

2.

3.

Week 1

Self-Care Plan

Self-care is one of the fundamental foundations of well-being. A self-care plan creates an understanding of the actions you need to take to support your emotional, physical, mental, work, and relationship well-being.

Your self-care needs are as unique as you are. There is no one-size-fits-all approach. That's why it's vital to identify your personal needs and create a plan that will work for you.

Benefits of self-care:

- Builds your capacity to manage stress
- Helps to maintain balance in your life
- Improves relationships
- Is unselfish
- Improves self-awareness
- Increases your capacity to care for others
- Helps you to feel more connected
- Builds resilience
- Decreases your risk of isolation
- Improves physical health
- Prevents burnout
- Improves understanding of self
- Increases positive thinking
- Boosts confidence and self esteem
- Positively affects mental health
- Enhances productivity

Step 1: Reflect and Identify

Reflect on the self-care actions that you currently have in place. Jot them down in the planner. You can use the list below the chart as a guide. Also note if there are actions that you would like to try.

Step 2: Consider

Consider the current self-care actions on your list.

- Which actions work well for you? Which ones don't?
- Which actions would you like to cultivate?
- Which would you like to reduce, change, or eliminate?

Step 3: Reduce, Change, or Eliminate

Now that you have identified what does and does not work well for you, categorise the actions into those that cultivate, those to change, or those to eliminate.

Current Self-Care Actions	Actions to Cultivate	Actions to Reduce/ Change/Eliminate

Self-care action suggestions

- Deep breathing
- Meditation
- Mindfulness practises
- Exercising
- Singing
- Dancing
- Good sleep habits
- Socialising
- Being a part of a support group
- Taking a bubble bath
- Listening to music
- Yoga
- Grounding
- Planning
- Journaling
- Being creative
- Reducing device/technology time
- Taking a break
- Asking for help
- Healthy eating habits
- Massage
- Walking in nature
- Saying no when applicable
- Using positive self-talk

Week 1

Reflections

_____

_____

_____

_____

_____

_____

_____

_____

_____

_____

_____

_____

_____

_____

_____

_____

_____

_____

_____

Week 2

Intentions

_____

_____

_____

_____

_____

_____

_____

Inspiration

The secret of getting ahead is getting started.

Mark Twain

Affirmation

I am motivated to create the life that I desire.

My Top Three Gratitudes

Monday

1.

2.

3.

Tuesday

1.

2.

3.

Wednesday

1.

2.

3.

Thursday

1.

2.

3.

Friday

1.

2.

3.

Saturday

1.

2.

3.

Sunday

1.

2.

3.

Week 2

Mindful Movement

Find a spot outdoors where you won't be disturbed. Walk slowly, mindfully aware of your senses—the smell of the grass, the sensation of your feet as they touch the ground, the sounds of the birds singing or the wind rustling the leaves on the trees, the warmth of the sun on your skin.

As you move mindfully, you may find your mind wandering; that is normal. Don't judge yourself. Just gently bring your attention back to your senses.

Week 2

Reflections

Week 3

Intentions

_____

_____

_____

_____

_____

_____

_____

_____

Inspiration

Happiness is a thing to be practiced, like the violin.

John Lubbock

Affirmation

I am fully present in all my relationships.

My Top Three Gratitudes

Monday

1.

2.

3.

Tuesday

1.

2.

3.

Wednesday

1.

2.

3.

Thursday

1.

2.

3.

Friday

1.

2.

3.

Saturday

1.

2.

3.

Sunday

1.

2.

3.

Week 3

Be Kind to Yourself

How do you speak to yourself when things don't go to plan? Are you kind to yourself, or do you beat yourself up?

When something doesn't go to plan or you make a mistake, how do you typically respond to yourself? What words do you use? What tone do you take?

_____

_____

_____

Imagine that you are responding to someone you love. What words would you use if he or she were having a hard time? If that person made a mistake? What tone of voice would you use?

_____

_____

_____

Is there a difference between the way that you respond to yourself and to someone you love?

Write down how things might be different if you responded to yourself in the same way you would to someone whom you love.

_____

_____

_____

Week 3

Reflections

Week 4

Intentions

_____

_____

_____

_____

_____

_____

_____

_____

Inspiration

Health is not just about what you're eating. It's also about what you're thinking and saying.

Unknown

Affirmation

I am full of gratitude and joy.

My Top Three Gratitudes

Monday

1.

2.

3.

Tuesday

1.

2.

3.

Wednesday

1.

2.

3.

Thursday

1.

2.

3.

Friday

1.

2.

3.

Saturday

1.

2.

3.

Sunday

1.

2.

3.

Week 4

STOP

Do you respond or react?

Practising the STOP mindfulness technique increases your automatic ability to pause between a stimulus and your reaction. It can also be used as a tool in the moment to create the pause.

S—Stop.

T—Take a few long, slow, deep breaths to anchor you in the here and now.

O—Observe the following without making judgements.

What are you seeing?
What are you sensing?
What are you feeling?
What are you thinking?

P—Proceed; now that you have created the pause, you are able to respond with appropriate and informed action rather than react from an uninformed place.

During the week, decide on three times each day that you can commit to practising the STOP technique. Set a reminder to prompt you to do so.

Think about times in your day that generally create moments of stress, such as being stuck in traffic, waiting in line, or having a conversation at work. Schedule your practise around these times so that you can experience the difference this makes in how you respond.

Week 4

Reflections

_____

_____

_____

_____

_____

_____

_____

_____

_____

_____

_____

_____

_____

_____

_____

_____

_____

_____

_____

_____

_____

Week 5

Intentions

_____

_____

_____

_____

_____

_____

_____

_____

Inspiration

Don't wait, the time will never be just right.

Napoleon Hill

Affirmation

I am unique, and I honour and love myself.

My Top Three Gratitudes

Monday

1.

2.

3.

Tuesday

1.

2.

3.

Wednesday

1.

2.

3.

Thursday

1.

2.

3.

Friday

1.

2.

3.

Saturday

1.

2.

3.

Sunday

1.

2.

3.

Week 5

Strengths

Have you ever stopped to think about your strengths? Maybe you've heard the saying, "Play to your strengths." Understanding and applying our strengths are integral parts in building our foundations for well-being.

There is much research in the field of positive psychology around strengths and well-being. When we use our strengths, we feel energised and more motivated. We feel more confident.

Take some time to think about situations in your daily life when your actions energise and motivate you. Notice throughout the week when you are, "Playing to your strengths."

Create a list of the energising and motivating strengths that you spot yourself using. Decide if you could bring those strengths to other situations in which you might experience challenges.

Week 5

Reflections

Week 6

Intentions

_____

_____

_____

_____

_____

_____

_____

_____

Inspiration

A journey of a thousand miles must begin with a single step.

Lao-Tzu

Affirmation

I live my life with confidence and courage.

My Top Three Gratitudes

Monday

1.

2.

3.

Tuesday

1.

2.

3.

Wednesday

1.

2.

3.

Thursday

1.

2.

3.

Friday

1.

2.

3.

Saturday

1.

2.

3.

Sunday

1.

2.

3.

Week 6

Explore your inspirations, and find meaning in your everyday world.

Step 1. Each day this week, take photos of the things in your life that you feel are meaningful, inspirational, or special to you. These things can be places, people, animals, objects, and so on.

Step 2. Each night, take some time to look back at the photos that you have taken. For each photo, reflect on how it is meaningful to you, how it inspires you, and why it is special to you. Write your reflections in your journal.

Week 6

Reflections

Week 7

_____

_____

_____

_____

_____

_____

_____

Inspiration

Our greatest glory is not in never failing, but in rising every time we fall.

Confucius

Affirmation

I am surrounded by love, hope, happiness, and health.

My Top Three Gratitudes

Monday

1.

2.

3.

Tuesday

1.

2.

3.

Wednesday

1.

2.

3.

Thursday

1.

2.

3.

Friday

1.

2.

3.

Saturday

1.

2.

3.

Sunday

1.

2.

3.

Week 7

Mindful Breathing

Set aside a few minutes each day this week to practise mindful breathing.
Get comfortable. This could be sitting up or lying down.

- Focus your awareness on your breath.
- Notice the sensations as you breathe in and breathe out. Or focus your attention on the rising and falling of your chest.
- If your mind starts to wander, gently shift your attention back to your breath.

Week 7

Reflections

Week 8

Intentions

_____

_____

_____

_____

_____

_____

_____

_____

Inspiration

The only way out is through.

Helen Keller

Affirmation

I face each day with a calm and flexible mind.

My Top Three Gratitudes

Monday

1.

2.

3.

Tuesday

1.

2.

3.

Wednesday

1.

2.

3.

Thursday

1.

2.

3.

Friday

1.

2.

3.

Saturday

1.

2.

3.

Sunday

1.

2.

3.

Week 8

Mindful Reminders: Coming Back
to the Present Moment

Set a reminder on your phone or decide on a cue. The cue could be when you receive a text message or are stopped at a red traffic light.

Each time you are prompted by your reminder or cue, take a mindful breath, pause before you react, become aware of your surroundings, and come back to the present moment.

Week 8

Reflections

Week 9

_____

_____

_____

_____

_____

_____

_____

_____

Inspiration

Who looks outside dreams; who looks inside awakes.

Carl Jung

Affirmation

I find joy and pleasure in the simplest things in life.

My Top Three Gratitudes

Monday

1.

2.

3.

Tuesday

1.

2.

3.

Wednesday

1.

2.

3.

Thursday

1.

2.

3.

Friday

1.

2.

3.

Saturday

1.

2.

3.

Sunday

1.

2.

3.

Week 9

Share the Gratitude

This activity is a great way to boost your positive emotions.

Think about a time when someone had a positive impact on your life through words or actions.

Write a thank-you letter to the person, detailing how his or her words or actions had a positive impact on you. Be specific. Write about the positive emotions that you experienced. Describe how these actions still create positive emotions in you.

If you want to increase the impact of this exercise, if possible, read your thank-you letter to the recipient. Or hand deliver the letter and be there when the individual reads it.

Take some time to write about this experience in your reflections.

Week 9

Reflections

_____

_____

_____

_____

_____

_____

_____

_____

_____

_____

_____

_____

_____

_____

_____

_____

_____

_____

_____

Week 10

Intentions

_____

_____

_____

_____

_____

_____

_____

_____

Inspiration

In order to carry a positive action, we must develop here a positive vision.

Dalai Lama

Affirmation

I release past anger and hurt, and I fill myself with loving and peaceful thoughts.

My Top Three Gratitudes

Monday

1.

2.

3.

Tuesday

1.

2.

3.

Wednesday

1.

2.

3.

Thursday

1.

2.

3.

Friday

1.

2.

3.

Saturday

1.

2.

3.

Sunday

1.

2.

3.

Week 10

Use Your Senses

Take time this week to notice when each of your senses is engaged and bring you positive emotions. It could be the smell of coffee in the morning, the sounds of children laughing, the taste of your favourite food, or the sight of a stunning sunrise.

Taking note of your senses is a great way of getting into the present moment and out of autopilot mode.

Smell	Taste	Sight

Sound	Touch

Week 10

Reflections

_____

_____

_____

_____

_____

_____

_____

_____

_____

_____

_____

_____

_____

_____

_____

_____

_____

_____

_____

_____

_____

Week 11

Intentions

Inspiration

All you need is the plan, the road map and the courage to press on to your destination.

Earl Nightingale

Affirmation

I take action, and I accomplish my goals.

My Top Three Gratitudes

Monday
1.
2.
3.

Tuesday
1.
2.
3.

Wednesday
1.
2.
3.

Thursday
1.
2.
3.

Friday

1.

2.

3.

Saturday

1.

2.

3.

Sunday

1.

2.

3.

Week 11

Raise Your Mood

Did you know that your posture can impact your mood? When you think of someone unhappy, how do you imagine the person's posture? Slouched over, head down, not smiling.

This week, use your posture to positively affect your mood. Stand tall, shoulders back, neck straight, and chin slightly lowered. Smile.

Imagine that your feet are planted firmly on the ground. There is a cable running through your body to the top of your head that is keeping you tall and straight.

Stand like this for about thirty seconds. Then take a short walk around the room, maintaining the posture and the smile.

Note in your reflections how this exercise affected your mood.

Week 11

Reflections

Week 12

Intentions

_____

_____

_____

_____

_____

_____

_____

_____

Inspiration

No act of kindness, no matter how small, is ever wasted.

Aesop

Affirmation

I am healthy, happy, and balanced.

My Top Three Gratitudes

Monday

1.

2.

3.

Tuesday

1.

2.

3.

Wednesday

1.

2.

3.

Thursday

1.

2.

3.

Friday

1.

2.

3.

Saturday

1.

2.

3.

Sunday

1.

2.

3.

Week 12

Checking In

Choose a cue, either a reminder on your phone or a physical cue, to remind you to check in every couple of hours throughout the day. During the day, at the reminder that you've set for yourself, stop what you are doing, and check in with yourself. What emotions are present? What physical sensations are you experiencing? Are your muscles tense? Are you on autopilot? Are you feeling happy?

Whatever you notice, take a moment to become aware of yourself. Just observe and allow.

Now, take a few deep breaths. Release any tension you may feel. Acknowledge your emotions.

What are your emotions and physical sensations telling you? Do you need to get up and stretch? Do you need to have a drink or something to eat? Do you need to challenge some negative self-talk? Or simply acknowledge the positive emotions that you are feeling.

Over the week, take note of how your awareness of your self increases as you continue to check in and increase your awareness.

Week 12

Reflections

_____

_____

_____

_____

_____

_____

_____

_____

_____

_____

_____

_____

_____

_____

_____

_____

_____

_____

_____

Printed in the United States
By Bookmasters